THE
Calvin and Hobbes
PORTABLE COMPENDIUM

BOOK 7

BILL WATTERSON

Andrews McMeel
PUBLISHING®

CaLViN aNd HobBEs

by WATTERSON

WOW, HONEY, YOU'RE MISSING A BEAUTIFUL SUNSET OUT HERE!

I'LL COUNT TO 10, AND THEN... *POW!*

DAD, HOW COME OLD PHOTOGRAPHS ARE ALWAYS BLACK AND WHITE? DIDN'T THEY HAVE COLOR FILM BACK THEN?

SURE THEY DID. IN FACT, THOSE OLD PHOTOGRAPHS *ARE* IN COLOR. IT'S JUST THE *WORLD* WAS BLACK AND WHITE THEN.

REALLY?

YEP. THE WORLD DIDN'T TURN COLOR UNTIL SOMETIME IN THE 1930s, AND IT WAS PRETTY GRAINY COLOR FOR A WHILE, TOO.

THAT'S REALLY WEIRD.

WELL, TRUTH IS STRANGER THAN FICTION.

BUT THEN WHY ARE OLD *PAINTINGS* IN COLOR?! IF THE WORLD WAS BLACK AND WHITE, WOULDN'T ARTISTS HAVE PAINTED IT THAT WAY?

NOT NECESSARILY. A LOT OF GREAT ARTISTS WERE INSANE.

BUT...BUT HOW COULD THEY HAVE PAINTED IN COLOR ANYWAY? WOULDN'T THEIR PAINTS HAVE BEEN SHADES OF GRAY BACK THEN?

OF COURSE, BUT THEY TURNED COLORS LIKE EVERYTHING ELSE DID IN THE '30s.

SO WHY DIDN'T OLD BLACK AND WHITE PHOTOS TURN COLOR TOO?

BECAUSE THEY WERE COLOR PICTURES OF BLACK AND WHITE, REMEMBER?

THE WORLD IS A COMPLICATED PLACE, HOBBES.

WHENEVER IT SEEMS THAT WAY, I TAKE A NAP IN A TREE AND WAIT FOR DINNER.

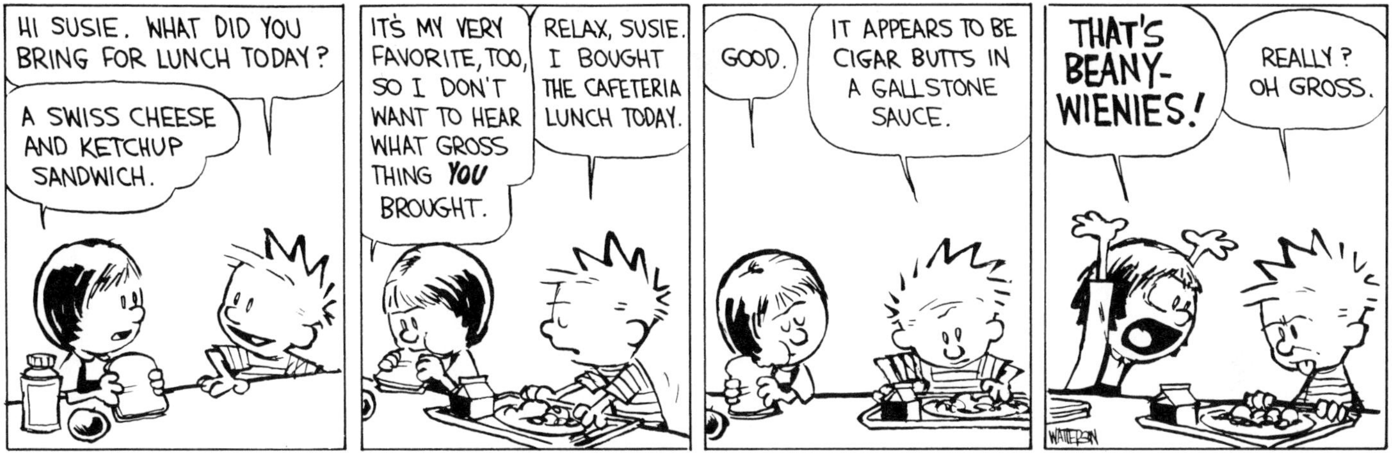
HI SUSIE. WHAT DID YOU BRING FOR LUNCH TODAY?
A SWISS CHEESE AND KETCHUP SANDWICH.
IT'S MY VERY FAVORITE, TOO, SO I DON'T WANT TO HEAR WHAT GROSS THING YOU BROUGHT.
RELAX, SUSIE. I BOUGHT THE CAFETERIA LUNCH TODAY.
GOOD.
IT APPEARS TO BE CIGAR BUTTS IN A GALLSTONE SAUCE.
THAT'S BEANY-WIENIES!
REALLY? OH GROSS.

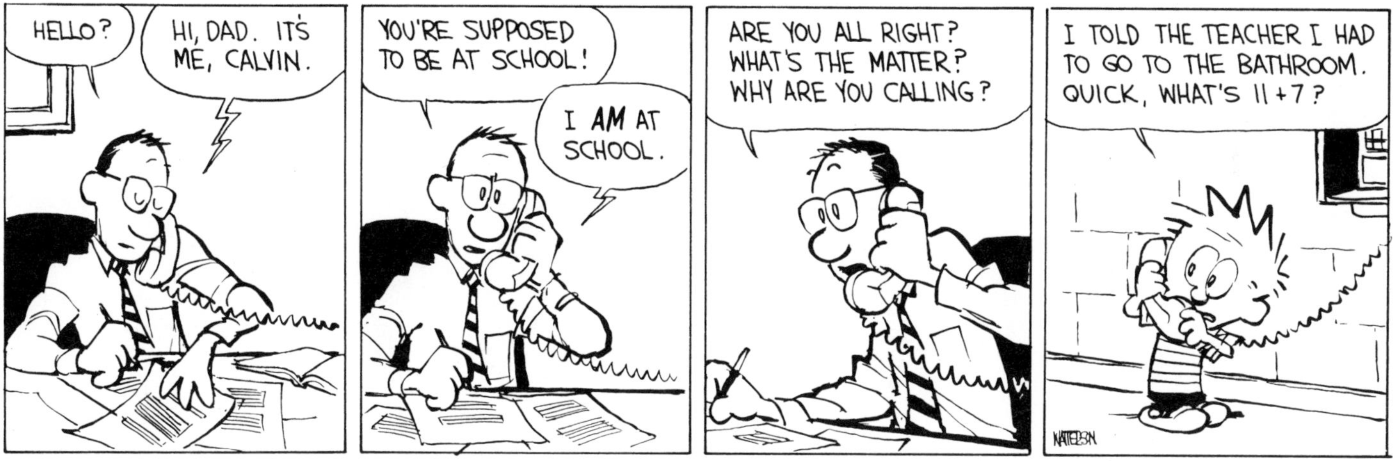
HELLO?
HI, DAD. IT'S ME, CALVIN.
YOU'RE SUPPOSED TO BE AT SCHOOL!
I AM AT SCHOOL.
ARE YOU ALL RIGHT? WHAT'S THE MATTER? WHY ARE YOU CALLING?
I TOLD THE TEACHER I HAD TO GO TO THE BATHROOM. QUICK, WHAT'S 11 + 7?

Calvin and Hobbes

by WATTERSON

CRIICKK

I SURE WISH IT WOULD SNOW.

WHAT'S WITH THE SLED? THERE'S NO SNOW.

I AIM TO FIX *THAT* RIGHT NOW WITH AN APPEAL TO THE SNOW DEMONS.

SNOW DEMONS?

OBVIOUSLY THEY'RE TORMENTING US WITH THIS WIMPY WEATHER BECAUSE THEY'RE ANGRY. WE MUST APPEASE THEM.

OH.

I'M GOING TO LIE HERE ON MY SLED AND THINK SNOW THOUGHTS UNTIL THE SNOW DEMONS HAVE MERCY AND UNLEASH A BLIZZARD.

SNOW, SNOW! HIGH AND LOW! WHEREVER WE GO! LET IT BLOW! TO AND FRO! HI-DE-HO! SNOW! SNOW! SNOW!

WELL, I'LL COME OUT IN EARLY JANUARY AND SEE HOW YOU'RE DOING.

TELL MOM I'LL NEED MY MEALS OUT HERE AND I WON'T BE GOING TO SCHOOL TOMORROW.

ALL THIS WIDE OPEN CEILING SPACE! I WISH I COULD GET MY ROLLER SKATES.

HEY, MAYBE I CAN CLIMB UP THIS BOOKCASE AND WHEN I GET TO THE BOTTOM SHELF, LEAP TO A CHAIR!

THEN I CAN PULL MYSELF ACROSS TO OTHER PIECES OF FURNITURE AND WORK MY WAY TO MY TOY CHEST.

...I CAN HEAR MOM NOW: "HOW ON EARTH DID YOU GET SNEAKER PRINTS ON THE UNDERSIDE OF EACH SHELF?!"

THERE! I THINK I CAN JUMP TO THAT CHAIR AND HANG ONTO THE BACK.

GEERONIMOOo!

¡WHOAAA!

WHAM!

GREAT. JUST GREAT.

CALVIN, QUIT BANGING AROUND!

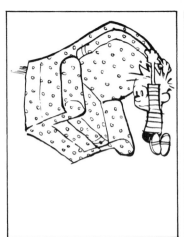

RRG!
MMF!

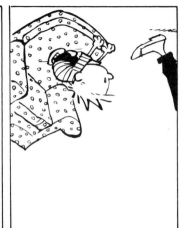

GETTING ANY *HOMEWORK* DONE, OR ARE YOU JUST RUINING FURNITURE?

MAYBE I'M HANGING HERE FOR DEAR *LIFE!* EVER THINK OF *THAT?*

I'M *TELLING* YOU, MY PERSONAL GRAVITY REVERSED ITS POLARITY! I FALL *UP* NOW!

I'VE BEEN TRAPPED ON THE CEILING! I COULDN'T DO MY HOMEWORK UP *THERE!* MY DESK IS ON THE *FLOOR!*

YOU SHOULD BE GLAD I WASN'T *OUTSIDE* WHEN IT HAPPENED, OR I'D BE SAILING THROUGH THE IONOSPHERE!

RIGHT. NOW I DON'T WANT TO HEAR ANY MORE NONSENSE UNTIL YOU'RE THROUGH WITH YOUR HOMEWORK, UNDERSTAND?

DON'T LET GO! DON'T LET GO!

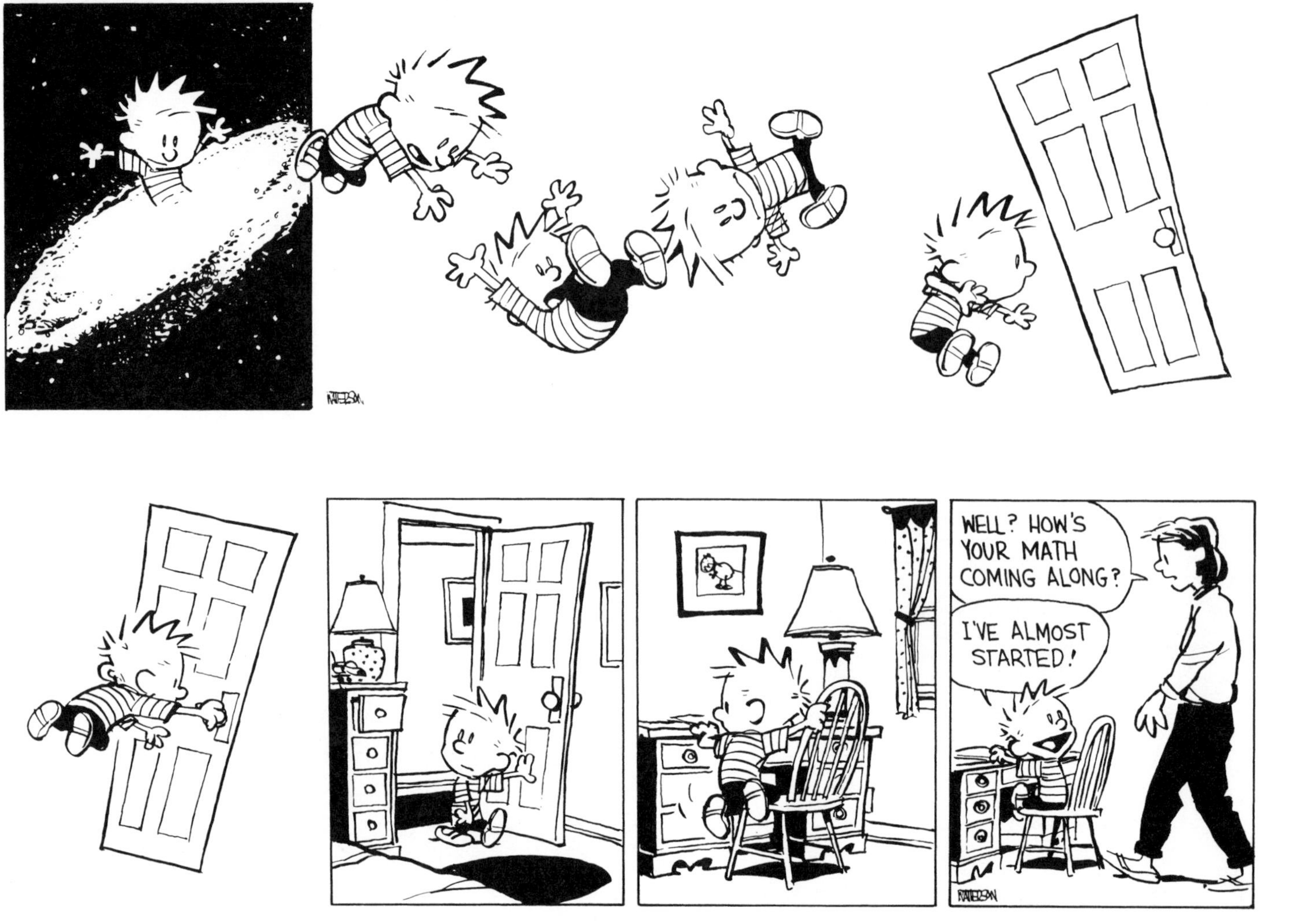
WELL? HOW'S YOUR MATH COMING ALONG?
I'VE ALMOST STARTED!

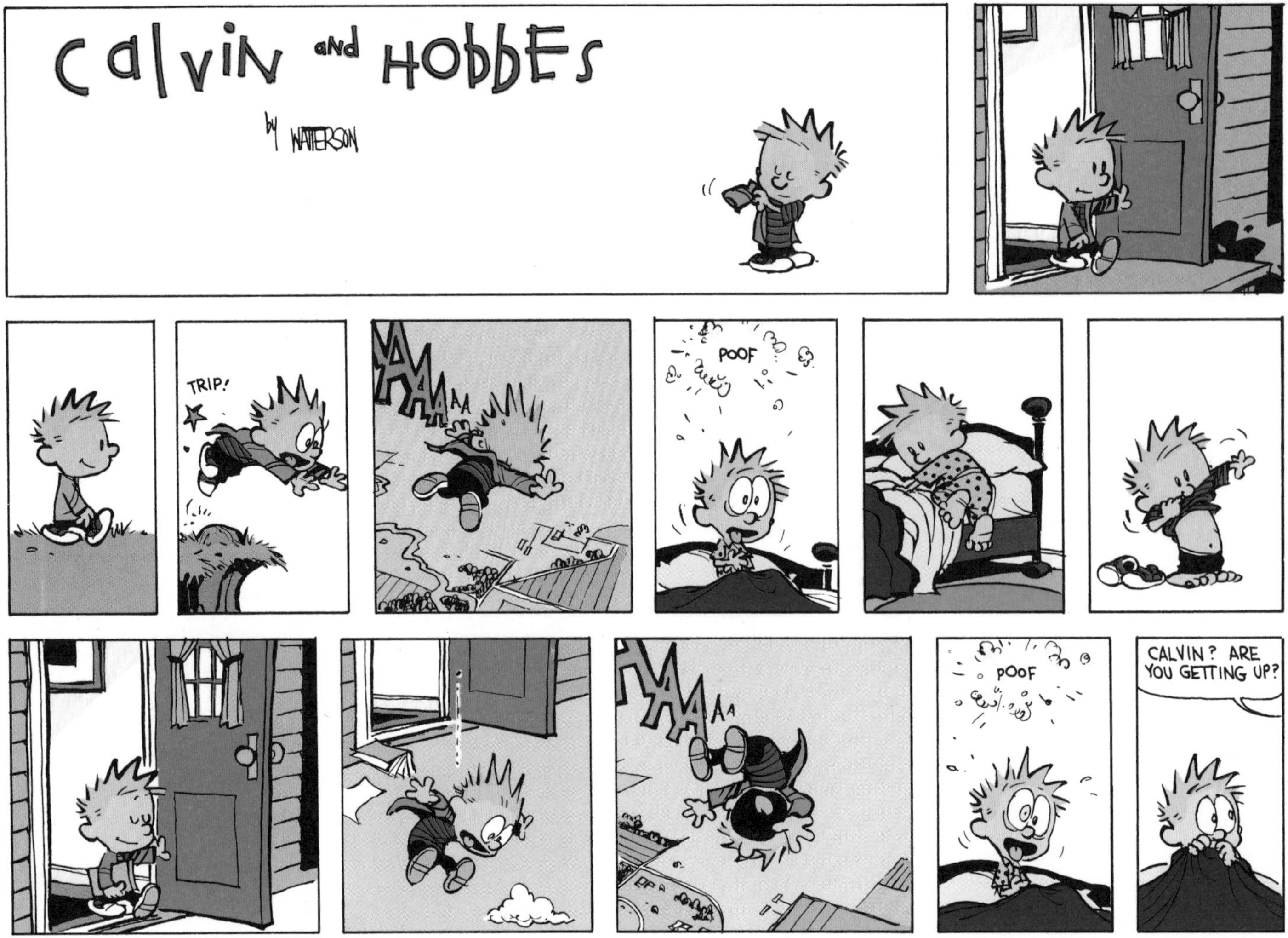
Calvin and HOBBES
by WATTERSON
TRIP!
AAAAAA
POOF
AAAAA
POOF
CALVIN? ARE YOU GETTING UP?

CALVIN and HOBBES

by WATTERSON

DEAR SANTA, HOW ARE YOU?

WELL, ENOUGH CHIT CHAT. LET'S GET DOWN TO BUSINESS.

THIS YEAR I WANT...

WILL YOU DRIVE TO WORK AND FAX MY CHRISTMAS LIST TO SANTA?

THAT'S A BIG ENVELOPE. ARE YOU MAILING A BOOK?

THIS IS MY CHRISTMAS LIST. CAN YOU BELIEVE THIS IS COSTING ME $2.40 TO SEND?

YES.

WELL, AT *THIS* PRICE, ALL I CAN SAY IS THAT SANTA HAD BETTER READ IT DARN CAREFULLY. LAST YEAR I DIDN'T GET HALF OF WHAT I WANTED.

HAVE YOU BEHAVED ANY BETTER THIS YEAR?

IT DEPENDS HOW YOU... *HEY, JUST WHAT ARE YOU INSINUATING?!* WHY, I'LL HAVE YOU KNOW I'VE BEEN A VERITABLE *ANGEL* THIS YEAR, JUST LIKE *ALWAYS!*

IN THAT CASE, WE CAN HAVE A COOKOUT WITH YOUR STOCKING CONTENTS.

DON'T GET SMART, BUB, OR I'LL WALLOP YOU ON THE 26TH.

DID YOU PUT ANYTHING ON YOUR LIST FOR *ME?*

WHAT, AND PAY MORE POSTAGE? THIS PACKAGE IS BREAKING MY ARMS ALREADY! GO WRITE YOUR *OWN* LIST!

TIDINGS OF COMFORT AND JOY TO YOU TOO.

LOOK, IT'S EVERY MAN FOR HIMSELF IN THIS WORLD. NOW GIVE ME A BOOST, WILL YA?

CaLviN and HObbEs

by WATTERSON

WHAT ARE YOU DOING STILL IN BED?! I'VE CALLED YOU THREE TIMES! YOU'RE GOING TO MISS THE BUS!

THAT'S THE IDEA. I'M STAYING IN BED UNTIL CHRISTMAS. I WANT TONS OF LOOT THIS YEAR, AND I FIGURE MY CHANCES OF BEING GOOD IMPROVE GREATLY IF I DON'T GET UP.

DISOBEYING YOUR MOTHER AND MISSING THE BUS ISN'T GOOD. IT'S BAD.

THAT DARN SANTA HAS GOT ME EVERY WAY I TURN.

I HATE THIS TIME OF YEAR. I'VE GOT TO BE GOOD FOR TWO MORE WEEKS IF I WANT ANY GOODIES THIS CHRISTMAS! I'LL NEVER MAKE IT.

I *TRY* TO BE GOOD! I *DO!* MY HEART IS AS PURE AS DRIVEN SNOW! IT'S JUST THAT, WELL, SOMETIMES EVENTS BEYOND MY CONTROL CONSPIRE AGAINST ME!

I'M USUALLY AN INNOCENT BYSTAND... HEY, I *SAW* YOU ROLL YOUR EYES! SO YOU DON'T BELIEVE ME, EH?!

ME??

BY GOLLY, EACH OF YOUR EYES WILL BE ROLLING TOWARD THE OTHER WHEN *I'M* THROUGH WITH YOU!

HA! I HOPE YOU ASKED SANTA FOR SOME CRUTCHES!

OOF.

ZING

BOY, IF IT WASN'T SO CLOSE TO CHRISTMAS, I'D POUND YOU GOOD!

YEAH, I'D LIKE TO SEE YOU TRY!

OH NO YOU DON'T! YOU'RE NOT TEMPTING *ME*! I WANT EVERY ITEM ON MY CHRISTMAS LIST, SO I'M BEING **GOOD**, NO MATTER WHAT THE PROVOCATION!

HERE COMES SUSIE DERKINS.

REALLY? QUICK, HELP ME FIND A PINE CONE I CAN THROW AT..

..*NO!* I'M BEING **GOOD!** GOOD! GOOD! GOOD!

YOU'LL NEVER MAKE IT TILL CHRISTMAS. GIVE UP NOW AND ENJOY YOURSELF.

HI CALVIN. ARE YOU BRINGING YOUR STUFFED TIGER TO SCHOOL TODAY?

NO, HE'S JUST KEEPING ME COMPANY WHILE I WAIT FOR THE BUS.

OH.

BUT ACTUALLY, HE'S BEEN NOTHING BUT TROUBLE TODAY. HE'S TRYING TO SABOTAGE MY CHRISTMAS BY MAKING ME BE BAD INSTEAD OF GOOD.

FORTUNATELY, I ASKED SANTA FOR SUCH GREAT PRESENTS THAT I CAN WITHSTAND ANY TEMPTATION. I'M BEING AN ABSOLUTE ANGEL.

WHAT DID YOU ASK FOR?

A HEAT-SEEKING GUIDED MISSILE. I FIGURE FIVE MINUTES WITH ONE OF *THOSE* BABIES WILL MAKE UP FOR THIS WHOLE ROTTEN MONTH.

CALVIN and HOBBES

by WATTERSON

'TIS THE SEASON TO ADVERTISE.

CALVIN, LOOK! YOU GOT A LETTER!

A LETTER? I DIDN'T HEAR THE MAIL TRUCK. A LETTER FOR *ME*?

THE RETURN ADDRESS SAYS "NORTH POLE".

OH MY GOSH, IT MUST BE FROM *SANTA*! SANTA SENT ME A LETTER! WOW! GEE!

READ IT! READ IT!

"DEAR CALVIN, YOU ROTTEN LITTLE KID..."

OH NO!! SANTA CALLED ME *ROTTEN*! I'M DOOMED!

KEEP READING.

"I MADE A LIST, BUT I DIDN'T BOTHER CHECKING IT TWICE, BECAUSE OBVIOUSLY YOU'RE THE NAUGHTIEST KID IN THE WHOLE WORLD."

AUGH!

WHAT ELSE?

"I'M WRITING TO GIVE YOU ONE LAST CHANCE. YOU'VE GOT SEVEN DAYS TO GET ON THE 'GOOD BOY' LIST."

SEVEN DAYS!! OH NO! WHAT CAN I *DO*??

MAYBE HE SAYS.

"I'D SUGGEST YOU START BY BEING KIND TO ANIMALS. PERHAPS YOU KNOW AN ANIMAL WHO WOULD LIKE A SNACK SOON. OR MAYBE YOU SHOULD LET AN ANIMAL READ YOUR COMIC BOOKS SOMETIME. THINK ABOUT IT."

SOUNDS LIKE SAGE ADVICE.

"SIGNED, SANTA CLAWS." *SANTA CLAWS?* WAIT A MINUTE! *I* RECOGNIZE THIS HANDWRITING! IT'S *YOURS*! SANTA DIDN'T WRITE THIS AT ALL!!

GIVE YOU A SNACK, HUH?! HOW ABOUT A KNUCKLE SANDWICH?!

HMPH. WELL, IT'S WHAT SANTA *WOULD'VE* WRITTEN IF HE WASN'T SO BUSY NOW.

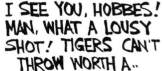
I SEE YOU, HOBBES! MAN, WHAT A LOUSY SHOT! TIGERS CAN'T THROW WORTH A..

SMACK!

I JUST THREW THE FIRST ONE SO YOU'D TURN AROUND.

A NEW DECADE IS COMING UP.

YEAH, BIG DEAL! HMPH.

WHERE ARE THE FLYING CARS? WHERE ARE THE MOON COLONIES? WHERE ARE THE PERSONAL ROBOTS AND THE ZERO GRAVITY BOOTS, HUH? YOU CALL THIS A NEW DECADE?! YOU CALL THIS THE FUTURE?? HA!

WHERE ARE THE ROCKET PACKS? WHERE ARE THE DISINTEGRATION RAYS? WHERE ARE THE FLOATING CITIES?

FRANKLY, I'M NOT SURE PEOPLE HAVE THE BRAINS TO MANAGE THE TECHNOLOGY THEY'VE GOT.

I MEAN, LOOK AT THIS! WE STILL HAVE WEATHER?! GIVE ME A BREAK!

calviN and HOBBES

by WATTERSON

HEE HEE HEE HEE

BUT FOR MY OWN EXAMPLE, I'D NEVER BELIEVE ONE LITTLE KID COULD HAVE SO MUCH BRAINS!

I'M A GENIUS, HOBBES. THERE'S SIMPLY NO OTHER WORD FOR IT. WHO ELSE WOULD THINK TO ARM A TOBOGGAN? IT'S JUST GENIUS!

SEE SUSIE DERKINS DOWN THERE? SHE'S BUILDING A SNOWMAN AND DOESN'T EVEN KNOW WE'RE UP HERE! WE'LL ZIP DOWN AND PELT HER SILLY WITH SNOWBALLS!

YOU STEER AND I'LL THROW! SEE, THE SNOWBALLS WILL GAIN EVEN MORE FORCE FROM OUR OWN VELOCITY! GENIUS, HUH?

HA HA! WE'LL BE A MILE AWAY BEFORE SHE CAN EVEN PICK HER HEAD OUT OF THE SNOW!

THERE SHE IS! STEER CLOSER SO I CAN GET HER! LEAN! LEAN!

AUGH! STEER! YOU'RE TOO CLOSE! MAYDAY!!

PIFF!

ANOTHER GENIUS THWARTED BY AN INCAPABLE ASSISTANT.

HEY CALVIN, LOOK UP.

CALVIN and HOBBES

by WATTERSON

I THINK THIS IS MY FAVORITE TIME OF YEAR! THE NEW SNOW MAKES EVERYTHING LOOK SO PRETTY.

WHOAAAAAA! WUMPH!

I THINK THIS IS MY FAVORITE TIME OF YEAR! THE NEW SNOW MUFFLES APPROACHING FOOTSTEPS! HOO HOO!

MAN, I CAN'T WAIT FOR SPRING.

QUIZ:
Jack and Joe leave their homes at the same time and drive toward each other. Jack drives at 60 mph, while Joe drives at 30 mph. They pass each other in 10 minutes.

How far apart were Jack and Joe when they started?

IT WAS ANOTHER BAFFLING CASE. BUT THEN, YOU DON'T HIRE A **PRIVATE EYE** FOR THE **EASY** ONES...

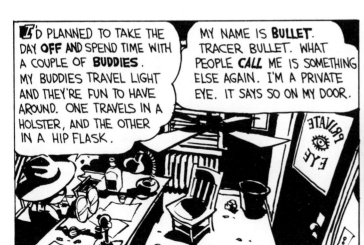

I'D PLANNED TO TAKE THE DAY **OFF** AND SPEND TIME WITH A COUPLE OF **BUDDIES**. MY BUDDIES TRAVEL LIGHT AND THEY'RE FUN TO HAVE AROUND. ONE TRAVELS IN A HOLSTER, AND THE OTHER IN A HIP FLASK.

MY NAME IS **BULLET**. TRACER BULLET. WHAT PEOPLE **CALL** ME IS SOMETHING ELSE AGAIN. I'M A PRIVATE EYE. IT SAYS SO ON MY DOOR.

THE **LAST** THING I WANTED THIS MORNING WAS A **CASE** TO SOLVE, BUT THE DAME WHO BROUGHT IT WAS **PERSUASIVE**. MOST DAMES **ARE**, SOMEHOW.

GET TO WORK, CALVIN.

I TOLD HER IT WOULD COST HER FIFTY GREENBACKS A DAY, PLUS EXPENSES.

I STEPPED OUT INTO THE RAINY STREETS AND REVIEWED THE FACTS. THERE WEREN'T MANY.

TWO SAPS, JACK AND JOE, DRIVE TOWARD EACH OTHER AT 60 AND 30 MPH. AFTER 10 MINUTES, THEY PASS. I'M SUPPOSED TO FIND OUT HOW FAR APART THEY STARTED.

QUESTIONS POUR DOWN LIKE THE RAIN. WHO **ARE** THESE MUGS? WHAT WERE THEY TRYING TO ACCOMPLISH? WHY WAS JACK IN SUCH A HURRY? AND WHAT DIFFERENCE DOES IT MAKE WHERE THEY STARTED FROM??

I HAD A HUNCH THAT, BEFORE THIS WAS OVER, I'D BE SORRY I ASKED.

FIRST I FIGURED I'D TRY THE DERKINS DAME. SUSIE AND I NEVER HIT IT OFF, ALTHOUGH OCCASIONALLY WE HIT EACH OTHER.

SUSIE HAD A FACE THAT SUGGESTED SOMEBODY UPSTAIRS HAD A WEIRD SENSE OF HUMOR, BUT I WASN'T GOING TO HER PLACE FOR LAUGHS. I NEEDED INFORMATION.

THE WAY *I* LOOKED AT IT, DERKINS ACTED AWFULLY SMUG FOR A DAME WHO HAD A HEAD FOR NUMBERS AND NOT MUCH ELSE. MAYBE SHE'S GOT SOMETHING ON JACK AND JOE. THE QUESTION IS, WILL SHE SING?

NO, I WON'T TELL YOU WHAT THE ANSWER IS! DO YOUR **OWN** WORK!

THE DERKINS DAME WASN'T TALKING. SOMEONE HAD GOTTEN TO HER FIRST AND SHUT HER UP GOOD. I KNEW SUSIE, AND CLOSING HER MOUTH WOULD'VE TAKEN SOME WORK.

I NEEDED A CLUE AND A DRINK. ONE OF THEM I KNEW WHERE TO FIND.

YOU'VE MADE ENOUGH TRIPS TO THE WATER FOUNTAIN. FINISH YOUR QUIZ.

SUDDENLY A GORILLA PULLED ME IN AN ALLEY, SQUEEZED MY SPINE INTO AN ACCORDION, AND PLAYED A POLKA ON ME WITH BRASS KNUCKLES!

YOUSE AIN'T GOIN' NOWHERE, FLATFOOT.

THE INSIDE OF MY HEAD WAS EXPLODING WITH FIREWORKS. FORTUNATELY, MY LAST THOUGHT TURNED OUT THE LIGHTS WHEN IT LEFT.

WHEN I CAME TO, THE PIECES ALL FIT TOGETHER. JACK AND JOE'S LIVES WERE DEFINED BY INTEGERS. OBVIOUSLY, THEY WERE PART OF A "NUMBERS" RACKET!

BACK IN THE OFFICE, I PULLED THE FILES ON ALL THE NUMBERS BIG ENOUGH TO KEEP SUSIE QUIET AND WANT ME OUT OF THE PICTURE. THE ANSWER HIT ME LIKE A .44 SLUG. IT HAD TO BE THE NUMBER THEY CALLED "MR. BILLION."

Answer: 1,000,000,000

CASE CLOSED!

TIME'S UP. BRING YOUR PAPERS FORWARD.

WHAT DID YOU GET, CALVIN? I THINK THE ANSWER'S 15.

SEE? **SEE?** STARBOARD IS **RIGHT!** PORT IS LEFT!

OK, SO I WAS WRONG FOR ONCE IN MY LIFE! SHUT UP.

AARGHH! I **MISSED!** IT'S THESE DARN FUZZY MITTENS! THE SNOW **STICKS** TO 'EM AND YOU CAN'T THROW STRAIGHT! DARN IT! DARN IT! DARN IT!

I **HATE** THESE FUZZY MITTENS! IF ONLY MOM HAD GOTTEN ME PADDED GLOVES INSTEAD OF THESE NO-GOOD, AWFUL, ROTTEN FUZZY MITTENS!

WHAP!

WELL I'LL BE! **MY** FUZZY MITTENS **HAVE** PADS!

WUMP!

ANY DUMB KID CAN BUILD A SNOWMAN, BUT IT TAKES A GENIUS LIKE ME TO CREATE *ART*.

THIS SNOW SCULPTURE TRANSCENDS CORPOREAL LIKENESS TO EXPRESS DEEPER TRUTHS ABOUT THE HUMAN CONDITION! THIS SCULPTURE IS ABOUT GRIEF AND SUFFERING!

ONE LOOK AT THE TORTURED COUNTENANCE OF THIS FIGURE CONFIRMS THAT THE ARTIST HAS DRUNK DEEPLY FROM THE CUP OF LIFE! THIS WORK SHALL ENDURE AND INSPIRE FUTURE GENERATIONS!

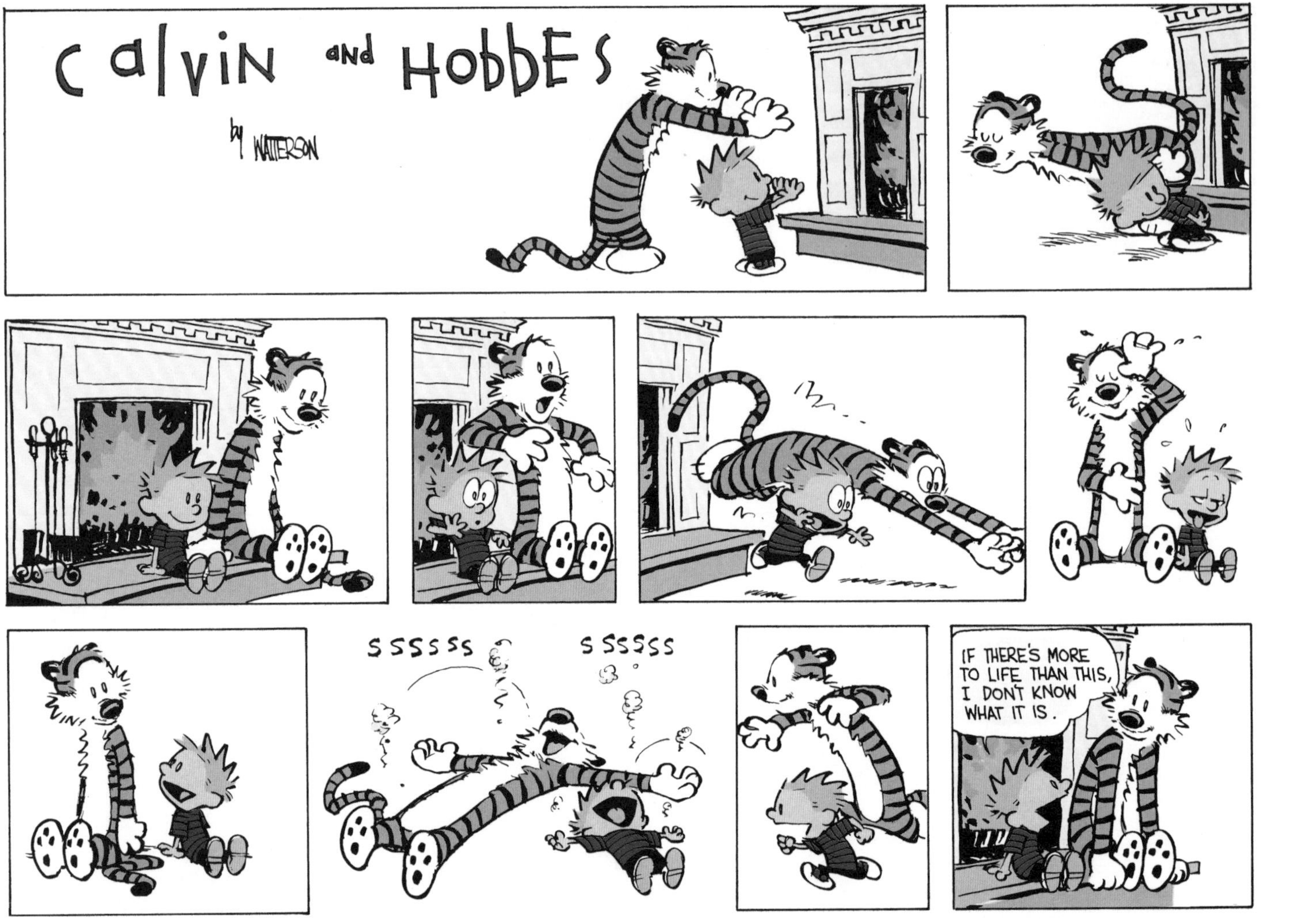
Calvin and HOBBES
by WATTERSON
SSSSSS
SSSSSS
IF THERE'S MORE TO LIFE THAN THIS, I DON'T KNOW WHAT IT IS.

140 MILLION YEARS AGO, THE INCREDIBLE 'ULTRASAURS' WANDER THE EARTH! SOME WEIGH OVER 70 TONS, AND EVEN THE VICIOUS ALLOSAURS ARE NO MATCH FOR THESE GIANTS!

BUT WAIT! A DISTANT RUMBLING SENDS THE ULTRASAURS INTO A PANICKED STAMPEDE! IS IT A VOLCANO? IS IT AN EARTHQUAKE?

NO! IT'S...IT'S A CALVINOSAURUS!

NAMED AFTER THE RENOWNED ARCHEOLOGIST WHO DISCOVERED IT, THE HUGE CALVINOSAUR CAN EAT AN ULTRASAUR IN A SINGLE BITE!

PHOOEY! I NEVER FIND *ANY*THING.

IT LOOKS LIKE YOU'VE HIT THE SEWER PIPE.

ONCE UPON A TIME, THERE WAS A...

HOLD IT.

YOU KNOW WHAT **ID** LIKE TO SEE? I'D LIKE TO SEE THE THREE BEARS EAT THE THREE LITTLE PIGS, AND THEN THE BEARS JOIN UP WITH THE BIG BAD WOLF AND EAT GOLDILOCKS AND LITTLE RED RIDING HOOD!

TELL ME A STORY LIKE **THAT**, OK?

AND HOW SHOULD HANSEL AND GRETEL MEET **THEIR** UNTIMELY DEMISE?

THE WITCH EATS THEM AND THEN THE WOLF EATS THE WITCH.

HEY DAD, CAN I TAKE THE GAS CAN FOR THE LAWN MOWER OUT IN THE BACK YARD?

WHAT ON EARTH FOR? IT'S 8:00 AT NIGHT!

I WANT TO POUR GASOLINE IN BIG LETTERS ON THE LAWN...

.. AND SET FIRE TO IT SO AIRPLANES CAN READ IT AS THEY FLY OVER!

NO, YOU CAN'T DO THAT! DON'T BE RIDICULOUS!

I DON'T EVEN WANT TO KNOW WHAT HE INTENDED TO WRITE.

CALVIN and HOBBES
by WATTERSON

BEWARE! FALLING BUCKEYES

HERE COMES SOMEBODY!

THIS MEETING OF THE TOP SECRET CLUB G.R.O.S.S. (GET RID OF SLIMY GIRLS) WILL COME TO ORDER. TODAY THIS AUGUST ASSEMBLY WILL DECIDE WHETHER TO DEMOTE PRESIDENT HOBBES ON CHARGES OF HERESY!

HERESY?!

LET THE RECORD SHOW THAT THE DEFENDANT MADE AN UNDISPARAGING COMMENT ABOUT THE POSSIBLE MEMBERSHIP OF SUSIE DERKINS, AN ADMITTED GIRL AND ENEMY OF THIS CLUB.

LET THE RECORD ALSO SHOW THAT SUPREME DICTATOR-FOR-LIFE CALVIN IS A NINCOMPOOP.

OK, JUST FOR THAT, YOU'RE ALSO CHARGED WITH INSUBORDINATION! THIS COURT FINDS YOU GUILTY ON BOTH COUNTS AND STRIPS YOU OF YOUR TITLE!

HA! AS COURT STENOGRAPHER, I REFUSE TO ENTER THE VERDICT! IN FACT, I'M PROMOTING MYSELF TO "EL TIGRE NUMERO UNO"!

OH YEAH?! WELL THEN, I PROMOTE MYSELF TO "MOST HIGHEST, GRANDEST, EXALTED, UM, SUPREME, UH..

THERE! I WROTE "HOBBES EQUALS GREAT" IN THE OFFICIAL CLUB NOTEBOOK! NOW IT'S A LAW!

HOBS = GRAT

IT IS NOT! GIMME THAT!

HA HA HA! I'M WRITING "HOBBES EQUALS UGLY FUR BALL"! WHAT DO YOU THINK OF THAT?

OH HO! I TAKE THE SUPREME DICTATOR HAT! NOW I'M THE SUPREME DICTATOR!

YOU GIVE THAT BACK!

I DECLARE YOU NULL AND VOID!

TRUCE? TRUCE.

WHAT A GREAT CLUB. TOO BAD WE DON'T HAVE MORE MEMBERS.

MAYBE WE SHOULD ALLOW SUSIE TO JOIN.

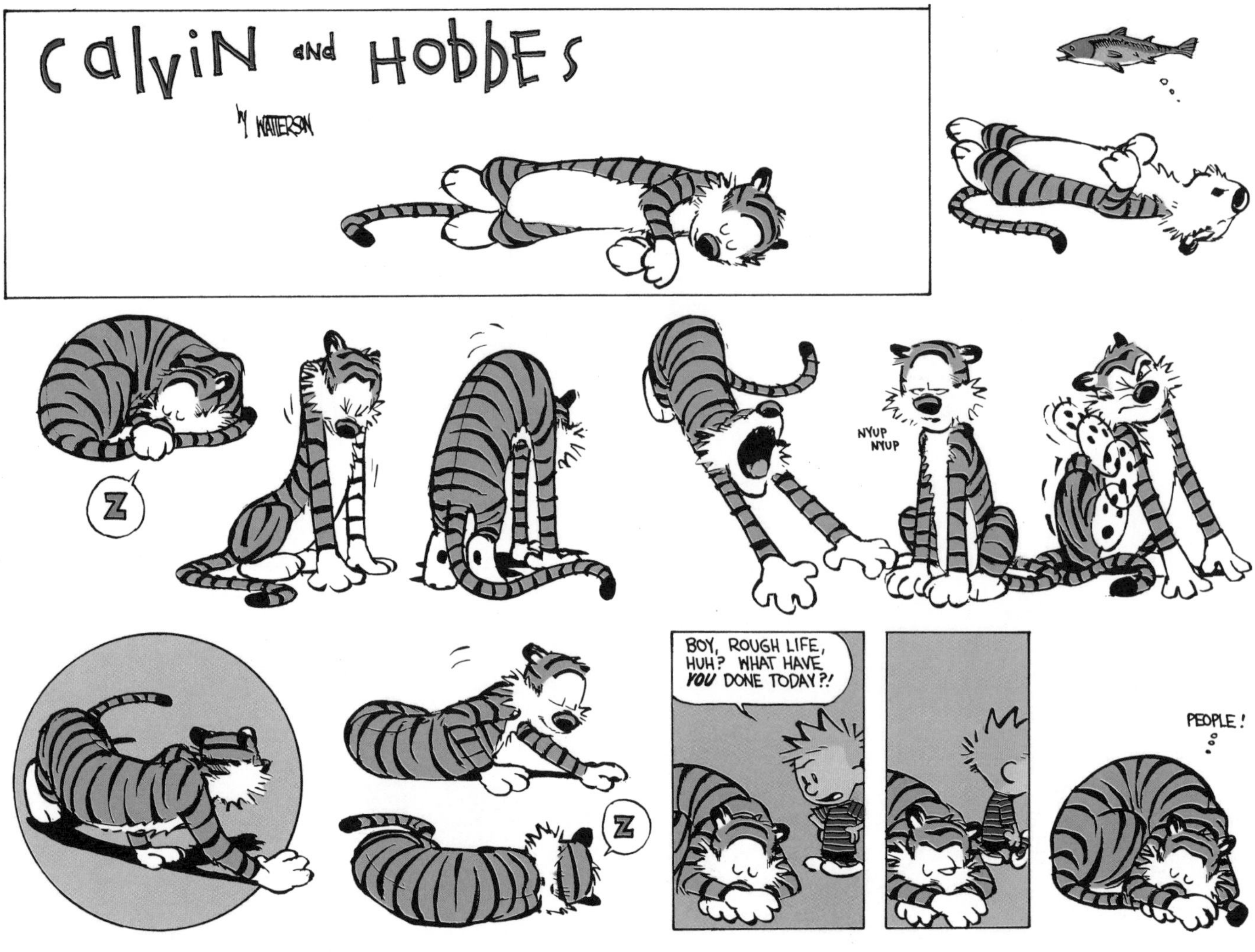
Calvin and HOBBES
by WATTERSON
Z
NYUP NYUP
Z
BOY, ROUGH LIFE, HUH? WHAT HAVE YOU DONE TODAY?!
PEOPLE!

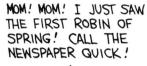

MOM! MOM! I JUST SAW THE FIRST ROBIN OF SPRING! CALL THE NEWSPAPER QUICK!

HA HA! A FRONT PAGE WRITE-UP! A COMMEMORATIVE PLAQUE! A CIVIC CEREMONY! ALL FOR ME! HOORAY! HOORAY!

OH BOY! SHOULD I PUT THE PRIZE MONEY IN A TRUST FUND, OR BLOW IT ALL AT ONCE? HA HA! I CAN'T BELIEVE I DID IT!

CALVIN...

IT'S A HARD, BITTER, CRUEL WORLD TO HAVE TO GROW UP IN, HOBBES.

CHEER UP! DID I TELL YOU I SAW A ROBIN YESTERDAY?

I SURE LIKE CHOCOLATE FROSTED SUGAR BOMBS! LOOK HOW BROWN THE MILK GETS!

UGH.

WANT TO SEE SOMETHING WEIRD? LOOK AT THE NUTRITIONAL INFORMATION ON THE BACK PANEL.

WOW. 100% OF THE DAILY RECOMMENDED ALLOWANCE OF CAFFEINE!

HEY LOOK! YOU CAN SEND AWAY FOR A CHOCOLATE FROSTED SUGAR BOMBS "BUZZY THE HUMMINGBIRD" DOLL!

CALViN and HOBBES
by WATTERSON

HMPH!

BOY, I'M IN A ROTTEN MOOD. THE WORLD HAD JUST BETTER LOOK OUT!

HEY YOU, YOU'RE IN MY WAY! MOVE IT!

WHAT'S THE MATTER? DID YOU GO DEAF?! GET OUT OF MY WAY! SCRAM!

C'MON, HURRY UP! YOU THINK I'VE GOT ALL DAY?!

NOW ARE YOU GOING TO STEP ASIDE, OR *WHAT*?! I'M COMING THROUGH!

MMPH! GGGHH! WHAT ARE YOU DOING?! I *SAID* MOVE ASIDE!!

DOGGONE IT, WHEN I SAY *MOVE*, I EXPECT YOU TO JUMP! *MOVE!*

MOVE! MOVE! MOVE! MOVE! MOVE!

HEY! PUT ME DOWN! WHERE ARE YOU TAKING ME?! I DEMAND AN EXPLANA... HEY, IS THAT A MUD HOLE?! YOU'D BETTER NOT! YOU HEAR ME?!

SEE WHY I'M IN SUCH A BAD MOOD?!?

DAD, WILL YOU EXPLAIN THE THEORY OF RELATIVITY TO ME? I DON'T UNDERSTAND WHY TIME GOES SLOWER AT GREAT SPEED.

IT'S BECAUSE YOU KEEP CHANGING TIME ZONES. SEE, IF YOU FLY TO CALIFORNIA, YOU GAIN THREE HOURS ON A FIVE-HOUR FLIGHT, RIGHT?

SO IF YOU GO AT THE SPEED OF LIGHT, YOU GAIN *MORE* TIME, BECAUSE IT DOESN'T TAKE AS LONG TO GET THERE. OF COURSE, THE THEORY OF RELATIVITY ONLY WORKS IF YOU'RE GOING WEST.

GEE, THAT'S NOT WHAT MOM SAID AT **ALL**! SHE MUST BE TOTALLY OFF HER ROCKER.

WELL, WE MEN ARE BETTER AT ABSTRACT REASONING. GO TELL HER THAT.

MOM, CAN WE GO OUT TO THE HIGHWAY?

DO WHAT?

SEE, I'LL PUT ON MY ROLLER SKATES AND TIE A ROPE FROM THE CAR BUMPER TO MY WAIST. THEN WHEN I GIVE YOU THE HIGH FIVE, YOU PATCH OUT WHILE I RIDE BEHIND AT 55 MPH!

WHAT DO YOU SAY? CAN WE GO?

I SURE WISH *YOU* COULD DRIVE.

CALVIN AND HOBBES by WATTERSON

ACE PILOT SPACEMAN SPIFF CRUISES LOW OVER THE PLANET AT HIGH SPEED!

I WONDER WHAT THIS "E" ON THE FUEL GAUGE MEANS.

THE INTREPID SPACEMAN SPIFF LANDS ON PLANET GORZARG-5!

OUR HERO SETS OFF ACROSS THE DESOLATE TERRAIN IN SEARCH OF HELP! IN THE DISTANCE, METHANE CLOUDS RAIN SODIUM HYDROXIDE, A CAUSTIC ALKALI!

OH NO! THE DOWNPOUR WAS TOO HEAVY FOR THE GROUND TO ABSORB! A STEAMING RIVER OF CORROSIVE LIQUID RUSHES TOWARD OUR HERO!

THE BRAVE SPACEMAN SPIFF SCRAMBLES TO HIGHER GROUND, BUT THE FLOOD CONTINUES TO RISE!

OUR HERO IS TRAPPED! IT'S ONLY A MATTER OF TIME UNTIL THE FOAMING, NOXIOUS WASH CLEANS THE MEAT FROM SPIFF'S BONES! HOW COULD THINGS EVER GET WORSE?!

AUGHH! AN ALIEN COMES TO PUSH HIM IN!

FOR HEAVEN'S SAKE, CALVIN! JUST GET IN!

I SIGNED UP TO PLAY BASEBALL EVERY RECESS, AND I DON'T EVEN *LIKE* BASEBALL THAT MUCH.

I MEAN, IT'S FUN PLAYING BASEBALL WITH JUST *YOU*, BECAUSE WE BOTH GET TO PITCH, BAT, RUN AND CATCH ALL AT ONCE. WE GET TO *DO* EVERYTHING.

MOSTLY WE JUST ARGUE OVER THE RULES WE MAKE UP! THAT'S THE PART *I* LIKE!

BUT THIS WILL BE WITH *TEAMS* AND ASSIGNED POSITIONS AND AN UMPIRE! IT'S *BORING* PLAYING IT THE *REAL* WAY!

DO YOU EVEN KNOW *HOW* TO PLAY THE REAL WAY?

SEE, THAT'S *ANOTHER* PROBLEM! SUPPOSE THEY MAKE ME A HALFBACK. CAN I TACKLE THE SHORTSTOP OR NOT?

I HEAR YOU SIGNED UP TO PLAY SOFTBALL AT RECESS.

YEAH, BUT I DIDN'T EVEN WANT TO. I JUST DID IT TO STOP GETTING TEASED.

WELL, SPORTS ARE GOOD FOR YOU. THEY TEACH TEAMWORK AND COOPERATION. YOU LEARN HOW TO WIN GRACIOUSLY AND ACCEPT DEFEAT. IT BUILDS CHARACTER.

EVERY TIME I'VE BUILT CHARACTER, I'VE REGRETTED IT! I DON'T *WANT* TO LEARN TEAMWORK! I DON'T *WANT* TO LEARN ABOUT WINNING AND LOSING! HECK, I DON'T EVEN WANT TO *COMPETE*! WHAT'S WRONG WITH JUST HAVING FUN BY YOURSELF, HUH?!

WHEN YOU GROW UP, IT'S NOT ALLOWED.

ALL THE MORE REASON I SHOULD DO IT *NOW*!

C'MON, LET'S GO OUTSIDE AND TRY SOME CATCHES BEFORE DINNER, OK? A LITTLE PRACTICE WILL MAKE YOU MORE CONFIDENT TOMORROW AT RECESS.

I HATE THESE FATHER-SON THINGS.

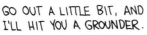

GO OUT A LITTLE BIT, AND I'LL HIT YOU A GROUNDER.

WHY DID I SIGN UP FOR THIS? I SHOULD JUST MOVE.

READY? NOW, BE SURE TO RUN UP TO THE BALL. DON'T JUST LET IT ROLL TO YOU.

ARE YOU OK? SOMETIMES THE BALL BOUNCES UP LIKE THAT, AND YOU'VE GOT TO BE READY.

THAGS FOR THE TIB, DAD. FIDE MY NODE AND PUD ID IN ICE SO THEY CAN SEW ID BAG OD!

GOODNESS, WHAT HAPPENED?! YOU WERE ONLY OUT THERE A MINUTE!

A GROUNDER BOUNCED UP AND HIT CALVIN IN THE NOSE.

I'B BLEEDIG! BY ODE DAD ID TRYIG TO GILL ME!

HOLD YOUR HEAD BACK, HONEY. HERE'S SOME MORE TISSUES.

I'B NOD PLAYIG BADEBALL EDDY MORE! NEBBER AGAIN! I HADE IT!

SIT STILL SO THE BLEEDING CAN STOP, OK?

I GUESS WE CAN FORGET HAVING A MILLIONAIRE BASEBALL PLAYER SUPPORT US IN OUR OLD AGE.

DEAR!

ALL BY CHARAGDER ID DRIPPIG OUT BY NODE!

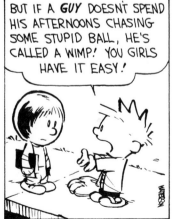

CALVIN and HOBBES by WATTERSON

I'M FREEEEEEEEEEEEEEEEEE

HO HO! THEY *TRIED* TO MAKE ME LEARN, BUT *I* WAS TOO *TOUGH* FOR 'EM!

I'M HOME!

WHY HELLO, CALVIN! DO COME IN, WON'T YOU?

CLICK.

HEY! HEY!

MAY I READ ALL YOUR COMIC BOOKS? I *MAY*? THANK YOU, CALVIN!

MAY I DRAW MUSTACHES ON ALL THE SUPERHEROES? I *MAY*? OH JOY!

I'LL GET HIM FOR THIS IF IT TAKES MY WHOLE LIFE.

Calvin and Hobbes
by Watterson

TOAD STROGANOFF!

..EWWWW..

POKE POKE

AUGH!

CLINK
CLINK
CLINK

HA!

SPLORPP!

SPLAT!

DON'T BLAME ME. I'M THE ONE WHO SAID WE SHOULD CALL FOR A PIZZA.

TODAY FOR "SHOW AND TELL," I HAVE A SOUVENIR FROM THE AFTERLIFE! YES, YOU HEARD RIGHT! EQUALLY AMAZING IS MY OWN STORY OF YESTERDAY AFTERNOON, WHEN I ACTUALLY DIED OF BOREDOM!

I WAS DOING MY HOMEWORK, WHEN SUDDENLY I COLLAPSED! I FELT MYSELF RISING, AND I COULD SEE MY CRUMPLED BODY ON THE FLOOR. I DRIFTED UP IN A SHAFT OF LIGHT AND I ENTERED THE NEXT WORLD!

EVENTUALLY, MY HEART STARTED AGAIN AND I CAME BACK TO LIFE... BUT NOT BEFORE BRINGING THIS BACK!

A YO-YO?

IT WAS PRETTY BORING THERE, TOO.

LET'S HAVE A LOOK AT THAT HOMEWORK.

AND SO, HAVING EATEN HER FILL, THE MOTHER BIRD RETURNS TO HER NEST...

..WHERE SHE REGURGITATES THE WORMS TO FEED HER HUNGRY BROOD.

...SIGHHHHHH...

CALVIN, PAY ATTENTION!

AUGH

THERE'S NO HEAD REST ON THIS CHAIR! I SHOULD SUE FOR WHIPLASH!

HEY MOM, DID YOU FEEL ANYTHING FUNNY WHEN YOU GOT DRESSED TODAY?

FUNNY? WHAT DO YOU MEAN?

WELL, TICKLY MAYBE... OR SCRATCHY? ANYTHING LIKE A BITE OR A STING?

WHY? AND WHAT HAVE YOU GOT BEHIND YOUR BACK?!

UM... HERE, YOU MAY WANT THESE. WELL, HEH HEH, GOTTA RUN!

WOMEN! ALWAYS CHANGING THEIR CLOTHES!

AFTER I GET THAT KID, YOU'RE NEXT.

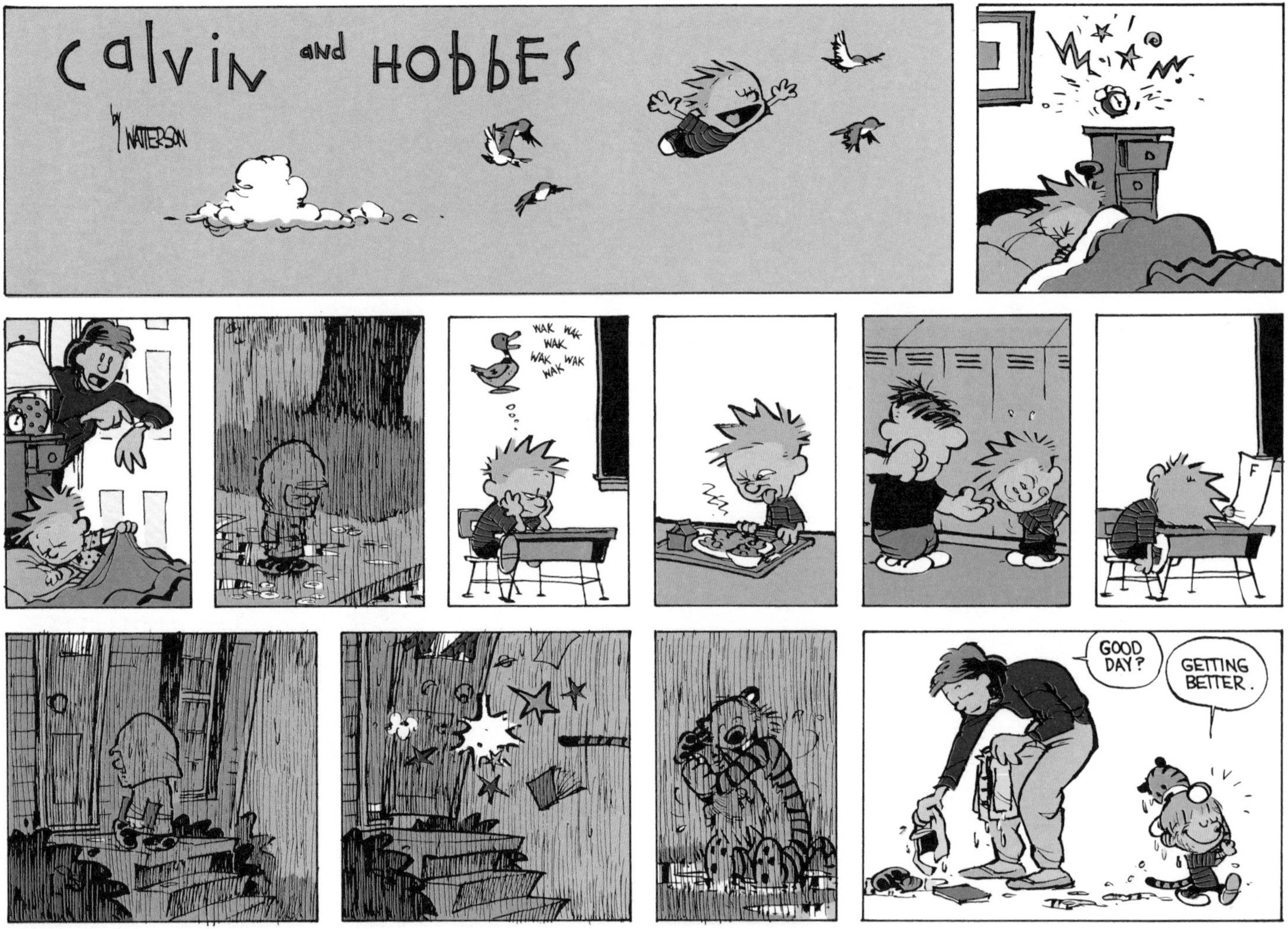
Calvin and Hobbes
by Watterson
WAK WAK
WAK
WAK WAK
WAK
F
GOOD DAY?
GETTING BETTER.

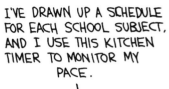

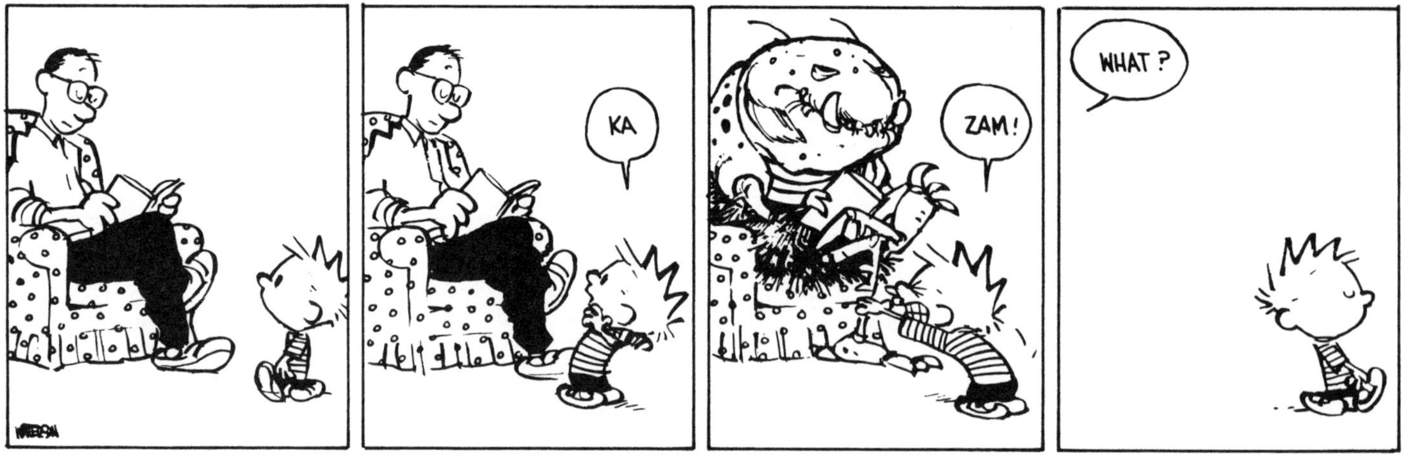
KA
ZAM!
WHAT?

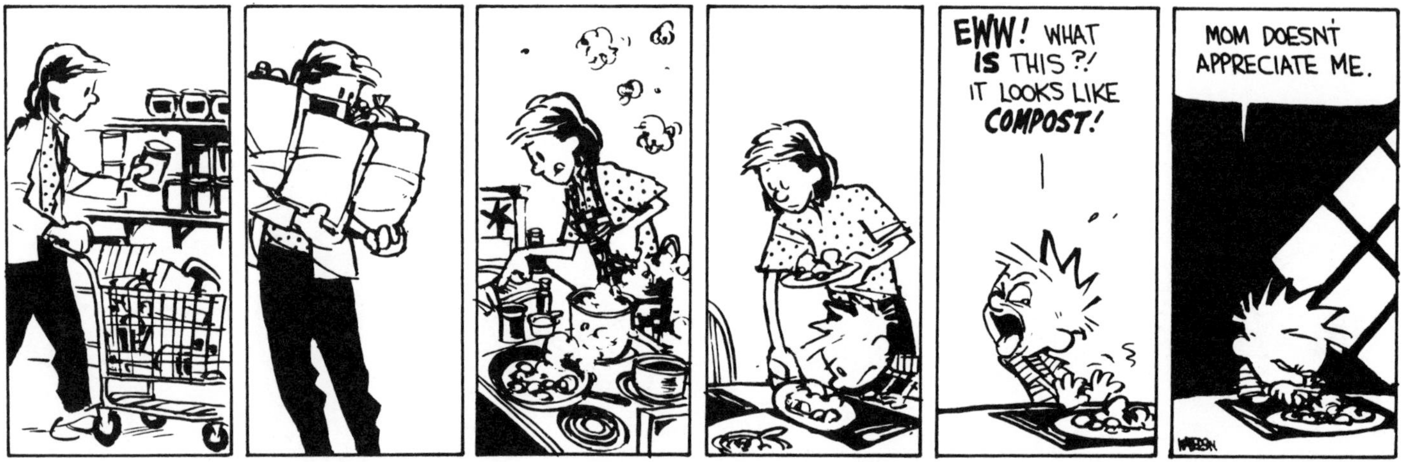
EWW! WHAT IS THIS?! IT LOOKS LIKE COMPOST!
MOM DOESN'T APPRECIATE ME.

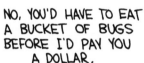

ANOTHER PLANET, ANOTHER SWEEPING PANORAMA OF INDESCRIBABLE GRANDEUR!

THE INCREDIBLE SPACEMAN SPIFF ZOOMS TO THE SURFACE OF AHNOOIE-4!

TOUCHING DOWN, OUR HERO SETS OFF TO SEARCH FOR SENTIENT LIFE!

ALAS, SPACEMAN SPIFF ONLY DISCOVERS A HIDEOUS BLOB SO MONUMENTALLY STUPID THAT IT JUST STARES STRAIGHT AHEAD, COMPLETELY UNAWARE OF ANYTHING AROUND IT!

COMPASSIONATELY, OUR HERO DECIDES TO PUT THE BLOB OUT OF ITS MISERY. SPIFF SETS HIS BLASTER ON "LIQUIFY."

EWW! MISS WORMWOOD! CALVIN'S SHOOTING SPIT BALLS!

PERPLEXED BY THE BLOB'S RESILIENCE, SPIFF ADDS MORE JUICE AND PREPARES TO FIRE AGAIN!

ON DISTANT PLANET ZARK, WE FIND THE EMPTY RED SPACECRAFT OF OUR HERO, THE BOLD *SPACEMAN SPIFF!*

UH OH! UP AHEAD, THE ROCKS ARE CHARRED WITH DEATH RAY BLASTS! A VIOLENT STRUGGLE TOOK PLACE HERE!

AND ONLY THE TRACKS OF A LARGE, SINISTER ALIEN LEAVE THE SCENE! WHAT HAS HAPPENED TO THE EARTHLING EXPLORER?

CALVIN, THIS IS HUMILIATING!!

I DON'T WANT TO GO! PUT ME DOWN!

SPACEMAN SPIFF IS BEING HELD PRISONER BY HIDEOUS ALIENS! WHAT DO THEY WANT WITH HIM?

SPIFF IS SOON TO FIND OUT! OUR HERO IS CALLED BEFORE THE ALIEN POTENTATE!

..WHERE IT BECOMES CLEAR THAT SPIFF IS ABOUT TO BE *SACRIFICED...*

..TO APPEASE THE EVIL GOD THEY CALL "NOLLIJ!"

UP TO THE BLACKBOARD. HURRY UP.

STARING DEATH IN THE FACE, OUR HERO THINKS FAST.

11 - 4 =

INCHING CLOSER TO THE SACRIFICIAL PIT, SPIFF SLOWLY AND SMOOTHLY REACHES FOR THE TINY ATOM BLASTER CONCEALED IN HIS BELT!

YAA! ALL RIGHT, YOU BLOODSUCKING, MUTANT CHROMOSOMAL DISASTERS! NOBODY MOVE! I'M OUTTA HERE!

CALVIN, GIVE ME THAT RUBBER BAND RIGHT THIS MINUTE!

I SAID NOBODY MOVE!

SPIFF ESCAPES! THE DANK AND SMELLY CORRIDORS OF THE ALIEN FORTRESS ARE DESERTED! ALL THE ALIENS HAD GATHERED FOR THE SPECTACLE OF OUR HERO'S DEMISE!

THE FEARLESS SPACE EXPLORER MAKES IT TO THE PLANET SURFACE, BUT THE ALIEN QUEEN IS IN PURSUIT!

CALVIN, GET BACK HERE!

SPIFF JUMPS INTO THE COCKPIT, PRESSURIZES THE LAUNCH THRUSTERS, AND...

BLASTS OFF! OUR HERO IS SAFE!

Tomorrow: OR IS HE??

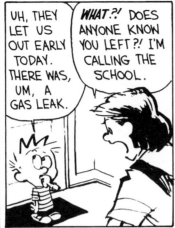

UFOs! ARE THEY REAL?? HAVE THEY LANDED IN OUR TOWNS AND NEIGHBORHOODS?

DO THE CHILLING PHOTOGRAPHS BY AN AMATEUR PHOTOGRAPHER REALLY SHOW A SINISTER ALIEN SPACESHIP AND THE GRIM RESULTS OF A CLOSE ENCOUNTER, OR ARE THE PICTURES AN ELABORATE HOAX?

LISTEN TO AN EXPERT ON SPACE ALIENS SPECULATE ON THEIR HIDEOUS BIOLOGY AND THEIR HORRIFYING WEAPONRY! ALL THIS AND MORE...

...ON CALVIN'S SHOW AND TELL ...NEXT!

CALVIN, WILL YOU COME HERE PLEASE?

TWITCHING TUFTED TAIL, A TOASTY, TAWNY TUMMY: A TIRED TIGER.

...AN ALLITERATIVE HAIKU BY CALVIN. THANK YOU, THANK YOU.

SHEESH.

YOU KNOW HOW PEOPLE LOOK AT MODERN ART AND ALWAYS SAY, "MY 6-YEAR-OLD KID COULD DO THAT!"?

WELL, THAT GAVE ME THIS GREAT IDEA! I'VE DECIDED TO BECOME A FORGER AND GET RICH PASSING OFF FAKE PAINTINGS TO MUSEUMS!

A LOT OF PAINTINGS SELL FOR TENS OF MILLIONS OF DOLLARS NOW, SO I MAKE A PRETTY GOOD HOURLY RATE.

YOU SHOULD PROBABLY SCRATCH OUT THE COPYRIGHT DATE ON THE CARTOON STATIONERY.

OOH YEAH, GLAD YOU CAUGHT THAT!

"ONCE UPON A TIME THERE WAS..."

HOLD IT. THIS STORY DOESN'T HAVE ANY SHOOT-UPS IN IT, DOES IT?

YOU MEAN GUNS? NO,

ANY VIOLENCE AT ALL?

UM... NOT REALLY.

ANY REFERENCES TO SATANISM? ANY PROFANITY? ANY CAR CHASES? ANY LEWD PARTS?

OF COURSE NOT!

WHAT MAKES YOU THINK I'LL LIKE THIS?

CALVIN and HOBBES

by WATTERSON

HISTORICAL MARKER
"CALVIN'S HOUSE"
IN JANUARY, SOME
40 SNOWMEN MET
A GRUESOME FATE
ON THIS SPOT.

EVERY DAY I LOOK FOR
A MOVING VAN HERE.

KNOCK
KNOCK

GREAT MOONS OF NEPTUNE!
A FOOL MORTAL FEMALE!

CALVIN?

I'M NOT CALVIN! I'M
STUPENDOUS MAN!
FRIEND OF FREEDOM!
OPPONENT OF
OPPRESSION!

UH HUH.
WHAT ARE
YOU DOING?

I WAS JUST ABOUT TO USE
MY STUPENDOUS POWERS TO
LIBERATE SOME COOKIES
BEING HELD HOSTAGE ON
THE TOP SHELF OF THE
PANTRY! NOW IF YOU'LL
EXCUSE ME, DUTY CALLS!

SLAM!

A BOLT OF CRIMSON STREAKS
ACROSS THE SKY! THE MAN
OF MEGA-MIGHT IS OFF TO
SAVE THE DAY!

DID THEY HAVE
AN EGG YOU
COULD BORROW?

NO ONE WAS
HOME, MOM.

CLICK.

PANDER TO ME!

PLAYING A RECORD? I'LL SHOW YOU SOMETHING INTERESTING.

COMPARE A POINT ON THE LABEL WITH A POINT ON THE RECORD'S OUTER EDGE. THEY BOTH MAKE A COMPLETE CIRCLE IN THE SAME AMOUNT OF TIME, RIGHT?

YEAH...

BUT THE POINT ON THE RECORD'S EDGE HAS TO MAKE A BIGGER CIRCLE IN THE SAME TIME, SO IT GOES FASTER. SEE, TWO POINTS ON ONE DISK MOVE AT TWO SPEEDS, EVEN THOUGH THEY BOTH MAKE THE SAME REVOLUTIONS PER MINUTE!

127

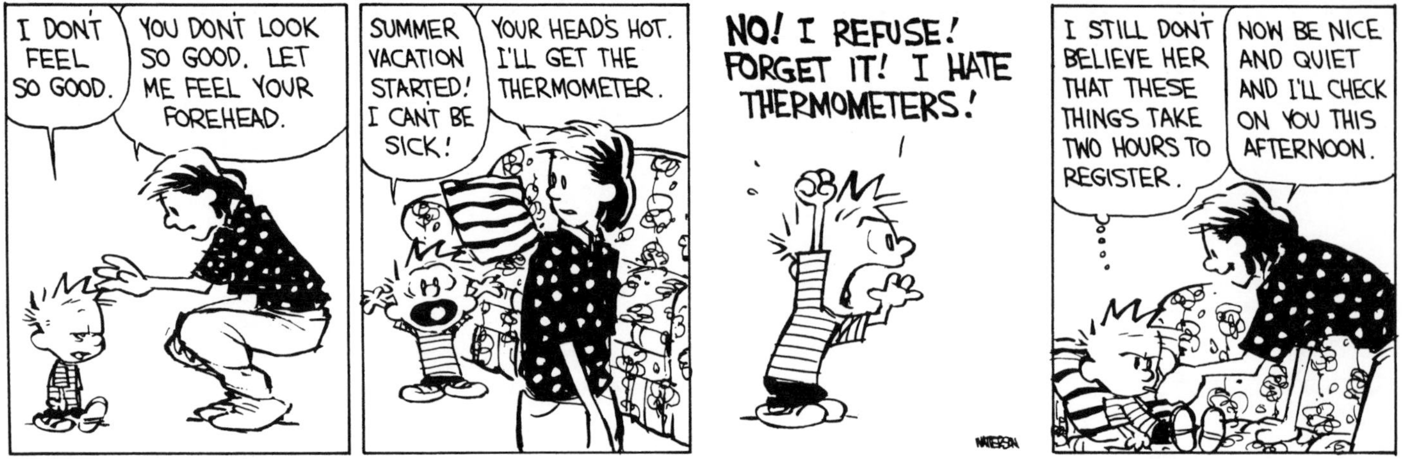
I DON'T FEEL SO GOOD.
YOU DON'T LOOK SO GOOD. LET ME FEEL YOUR FOREHEAD.
SUMMER VACATION STARTED! I CAN'T BE SICK!
YOUR HEAD'S HOT. I'LL GET THE THERMOMETER.
NO! I REFUSE! FORGET IT! I HATE THERMOMETERS!
I STILL DON'T BELIEVE HER THAT THESE THINGS TAKE TWO HOURS TO REGISTER.
NOW BE NICE AND QUIET AND I'LL CHECK ON YOU THIS AFTERNOON.

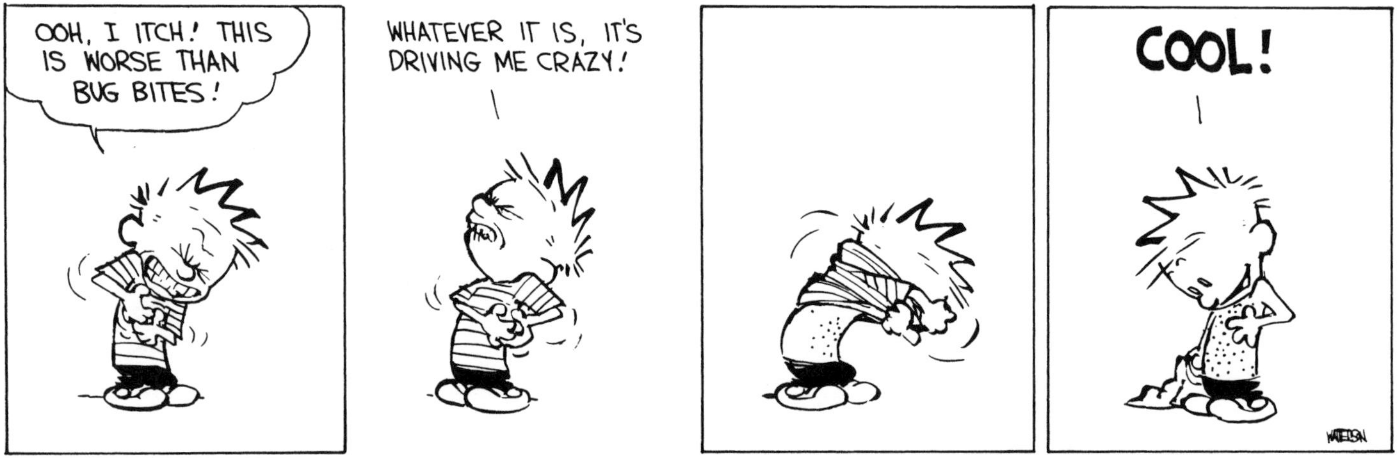
OOH, I ITCH! THIS IS WORSE THAN BUG BITES!
WHATEVER IT IS, IT'S DRIVING ME CRAZY!
COOL!

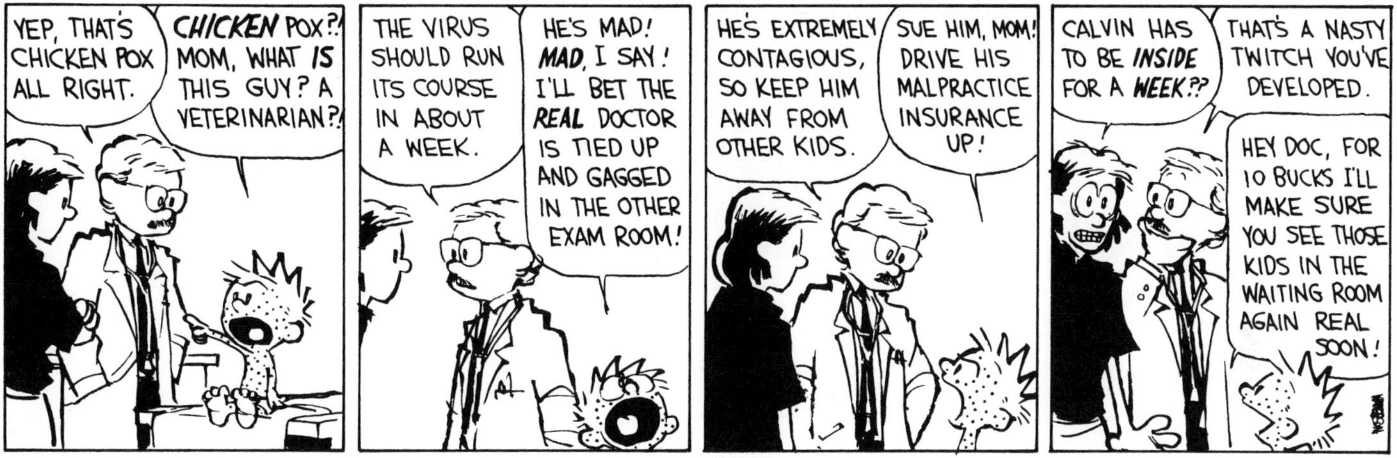
YEP, THAT'S CHICKEN POX ALL RIGHT.
CHICKEN POX?! MOM, WHAT IS THIS GUY? A VETERINARIAN?!
THE VIRUS SHOULD RUN ITS COURSE IN ABOUT A WEEK.
HE'S MAD! MAD, I SAY! I'LL BET THE REAL DOCTOR IS TIED UP AND GAGGED IN THE OTHER EXAM ROOM!
HE'S EXTREMELY CONTAGIOUS, SO KEEP HIM AWAY FROM OTHER KIDS.
SUE HIM, MOM! DRIVE HIS MALPRACTICE INSURANCE UP!
CALVIN HAS TO BE INSIDE FOR A WEEK??
THAT'S A NASTY TWITCH YOU'VE DEVELOPED.
HEY DOC, FOR 10 BUCKS I'LL MAKE SURE YOU SEE THOSE KIDS IN THE WAITING ROOM AGAIN REAL SOON!

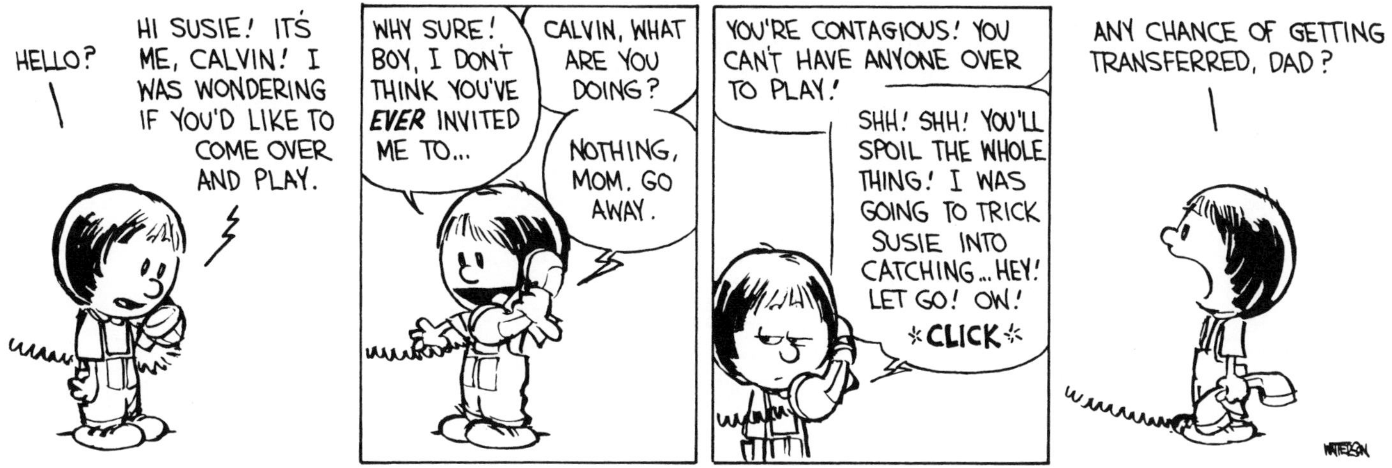
HELLO?
HI SUSIE! IT'S ME, CALVIN! I WAS WONDERING IF YOU'D LIKE TO COME OVER AND PLAY.
WHY SURE! BOY, I DON'T THINK YOU'VE EVER INVITED ME TO...
CALVIN, WHAT ARE YOU DOING?
NOTHING, MOM. GO AWAY.
YOU'RE CONTAGIOUS! YOU CAN'T HAVE ANYONE OVER TO PLAY!
SHH! SHH! YOU'LL SPOIL THE WHOLE THING! I WAS GOING TO TRICK SUSIE INTO CATCHING... HEY! LET GO! OW!
CLICK
ANY CHANCE OF GETTING TRANSFERRED, DAD?
WATTERSON

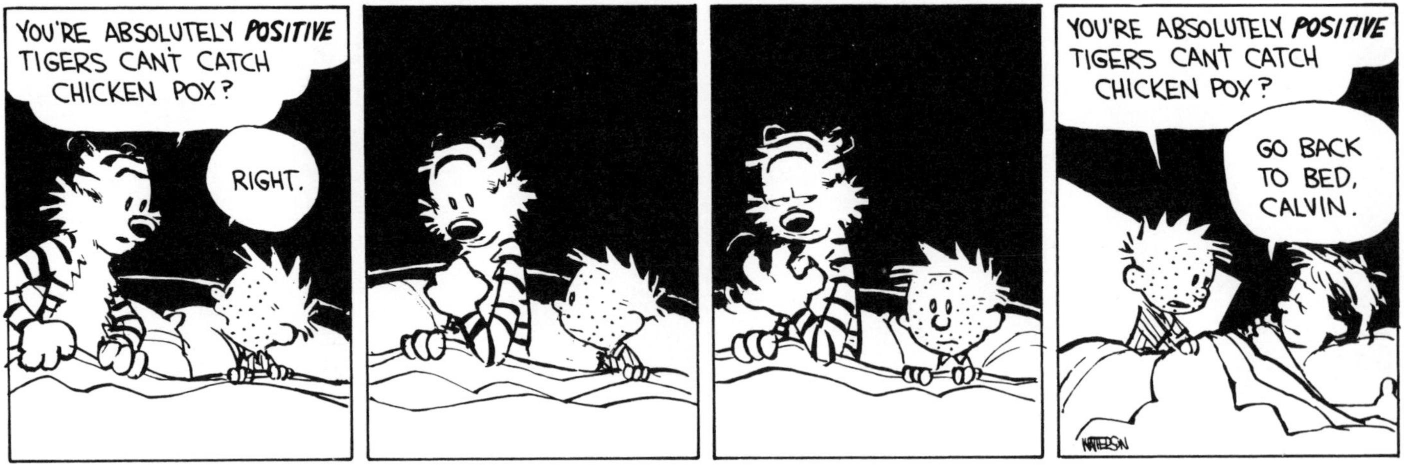
YOU'RE ABSOLUTELY POSITIVE TIGERS CAN'T CATCH CHICKEN POX?
RIGHT.
YOU'RE ABSOLUTELY POSITIVE TIGERS CAN'T CATCH CHICKEN POX?
GO BACK TO BED, CALVIN.

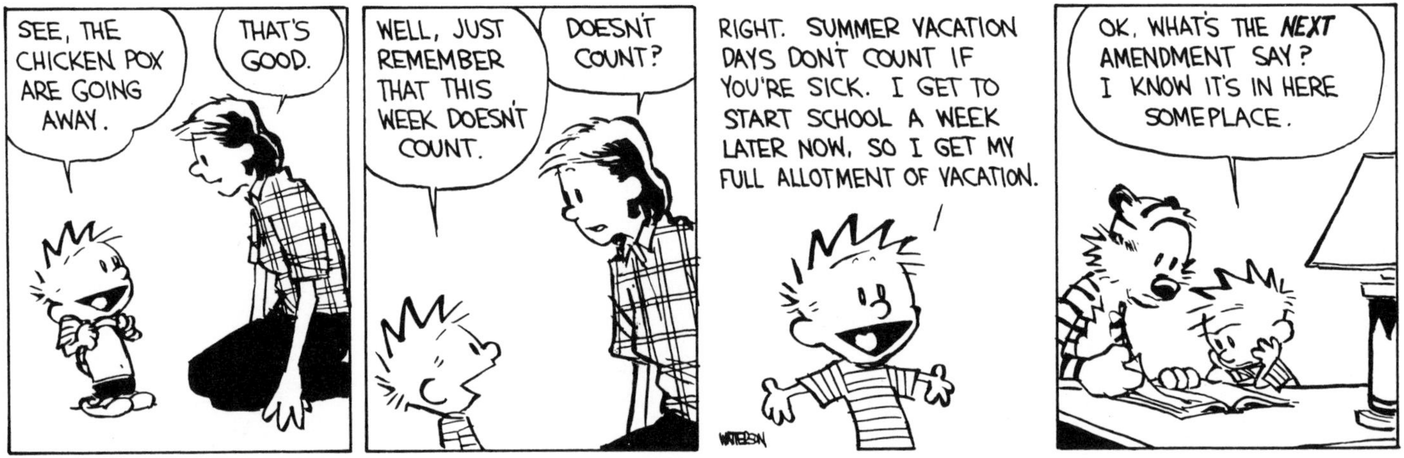
SEE, THE CHICKEN POX ARE GOING AWAY.
THAT'S GOOD.
WELL, JUST REMEMBER THAT THIS WEEK DOESN'T COUNT.
DOESN'T COUNT?
RIGHT. SUMMER VACATION DAYS DON'T COUNT IF YOU'RE SICK. I GET TO START SCHOOL A WEEK LATER NOW, SO I GET MY FULL ALLOTMENT OF VACATION.
OK, WHAT'S THE NEXT AMENDMENT SAY? I KNOW IT'S IN HERE SOMEPLACE.

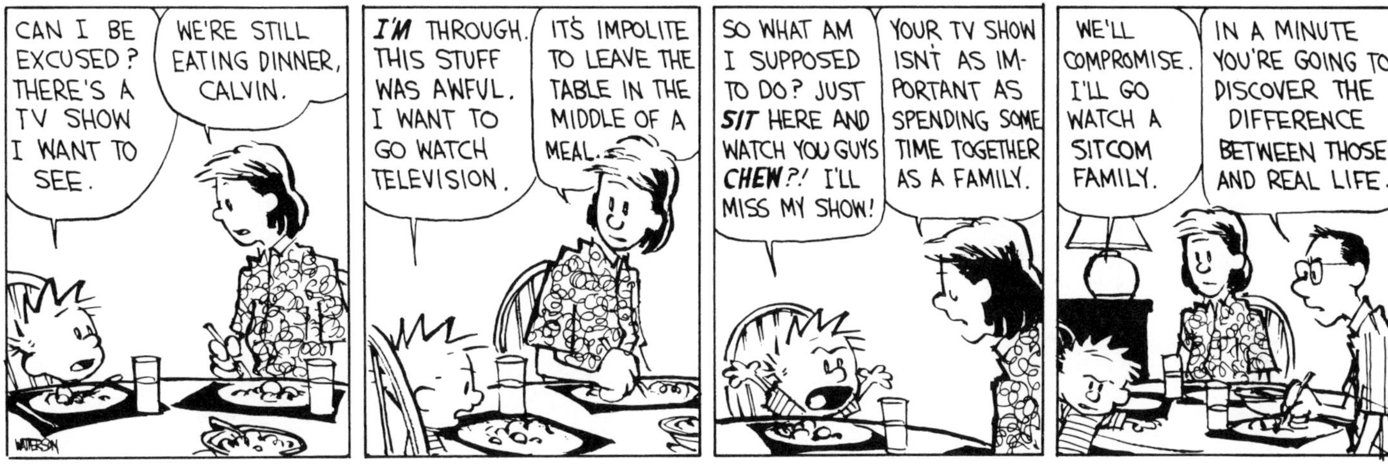
CAN I BE EXCUSED? THERE'S A TV SHOW I WANT TO SEE.
WE'RE STILL EATING DINNER, CALVIN.
I'M THROUGH. THIS STUFF WAS AWFUL. I WANT TO GO WATCH TELEVISION.
IT'S IMPOLITE TO LEAVE THE TABLE IN THE MIDDLE OF A MEAL.
SO WHAT AM I SUPPOSED TO DO? JUST SIT HERE AND WATCH YOU GUYS CHEW?! I'LL MISS MY SHOW!
YOUR TV SHOW ISN'T AS IMPORTANT AS SPENDING SOME TIME TOGETHER AS A FAMILY.
WE'LL COMPROMISE. I'LL GO WATCH A SITCOM FAMILY.
IN A MINUTE YOU'RE GOING TO DISCOVER THE DIFFERENCE BETWEEN THOSE AND REAL LIFE.

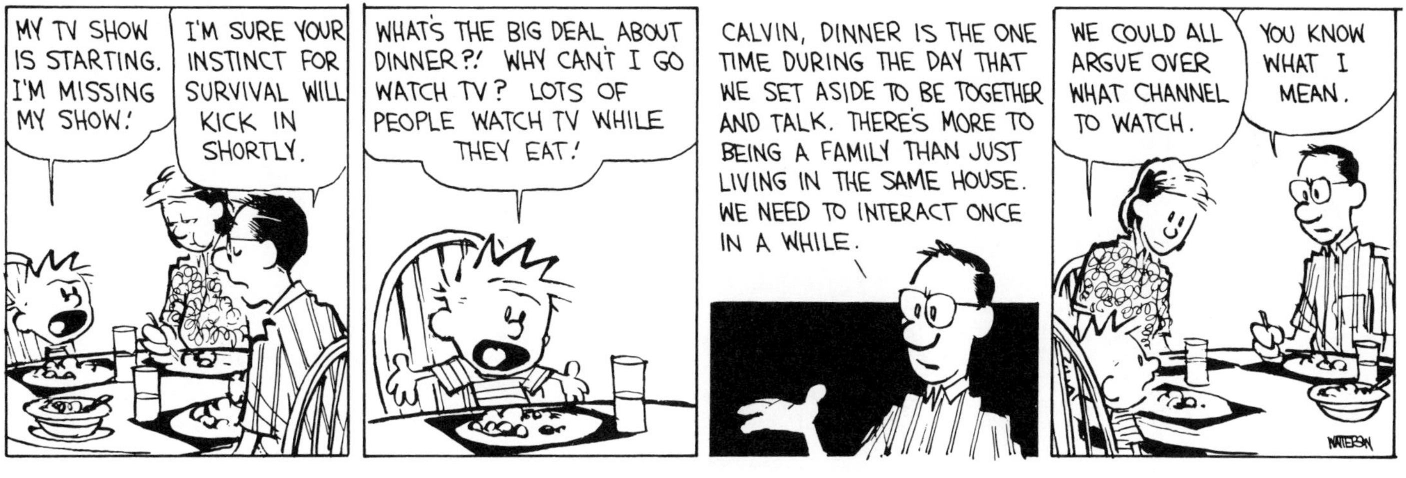
MY TV SHOW IS STARTING. I'M MISSING MY SHOW!
I'M SURE YOUR INSTINCT FOR SURVIVAL WILL KICK IN SHORTLY.
WHAT'S THE BIG DEAL ABOUT DINNER?! WHY CAN'T I GO WATCH TV? LOTS OF PEOPLE WATCH TV WHILE THEY EAT!
CALVIN, DINNER IS THE ONE TIME DURING THE DAY THAT WE SET ASIDE TO BE TOGETHER AND TALK. THERE'S MORE TO BEING A FAMILY THAN JUST LIVING IN THE SAME HOUSE. WE NEED TO INTERACT ONCE IN A WHILE.
WE COULD ALL ARGUE OVER WHAT CHANNEL TO WATCH.
YOU KNOW WHAT I MEAN.

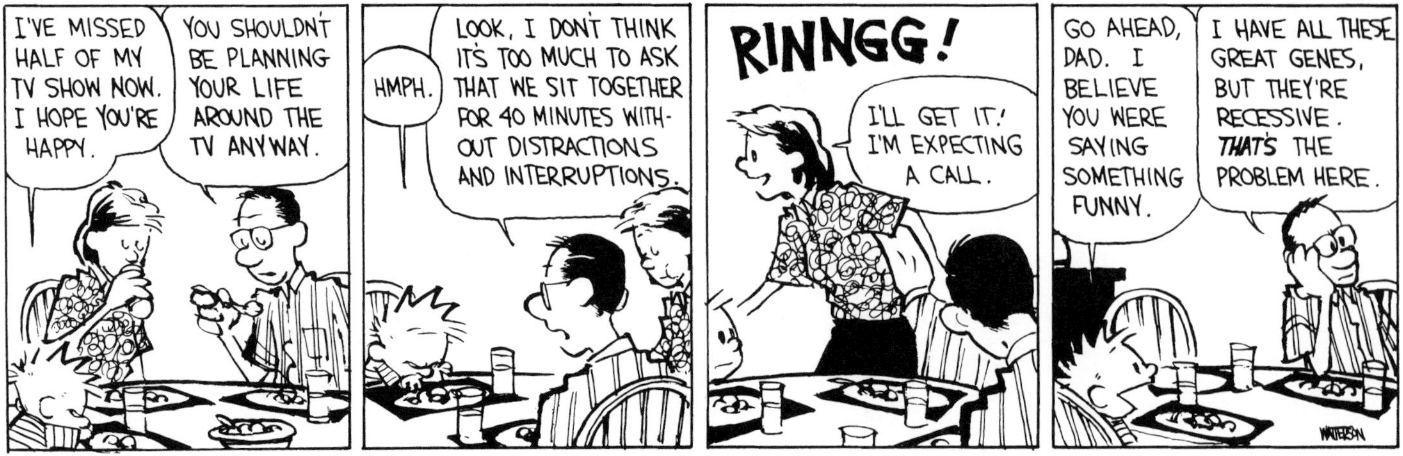
I'VE MISSED HALF OF MY TV SHOW NOW. I HOPE YOU'RE HAPPY.
YOU SHOULDN'T BE PLANNING YOUR LIFE AROUND THE TV ANYWAY.
HMPH.
LOOK, I DON'T THINK IT'S TOO MUCH TO ASK THAT WE SIT TOGETHER FOR 40 MINUTES WITHOUT DISTRACTIONS AND INTERRUPTIONS.
RINNGG!
I'LL GET IT! I'M EXPECTING A CALL.
GO AHEAD, DAD. I BELIEVE YOU WERE SAYING SOMETHING FUNNY.
I HAVE ALL THESE GREAT GENES, BUT THEY'RE RECESSIVE. THAT'S THE PROBLEM HERE.
WATTERSON

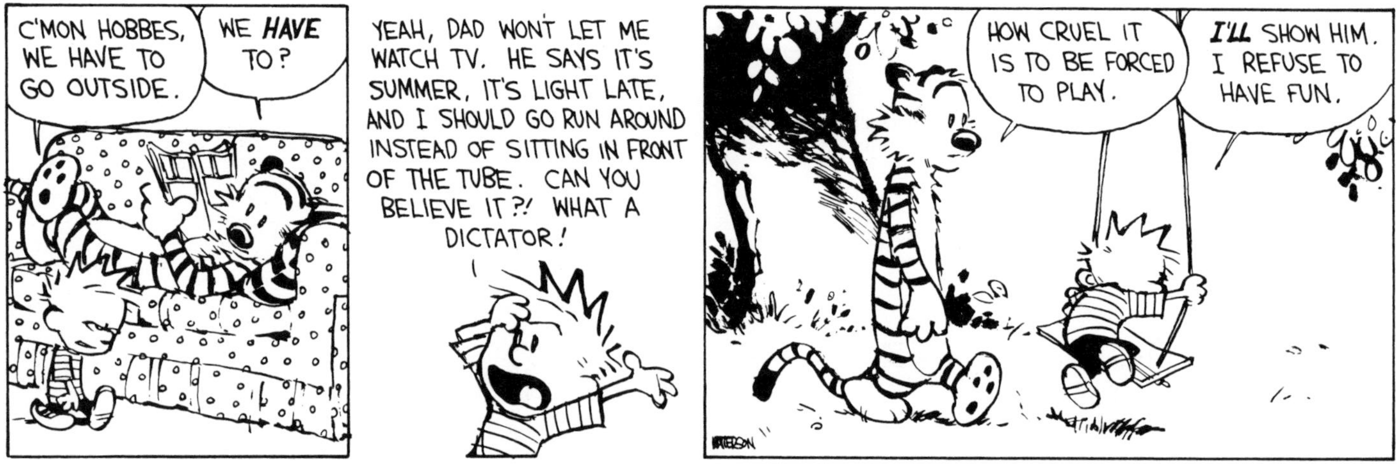
C'MON HOBBES, WE HAVE TO GO OUTSIDE.
WE HAVE TO?
YEAH, DAD WON'T LET ME WATCH TV. HE SAYS IT'S SUMMER, IT'S LIGHT LATE, AND I SHOULD GO RUN AROUND INSTEAD OF SITTING IN FRONT OF THE TUBE. CAN YOU BELIEVE IT?! WHAT A DICTATOR!
HOW CRUEL IT IS TO BE FORCED TO PLAY.
I'LL SHOW HIM. I REFUSE TO HAVE FUN.
WATTERSON

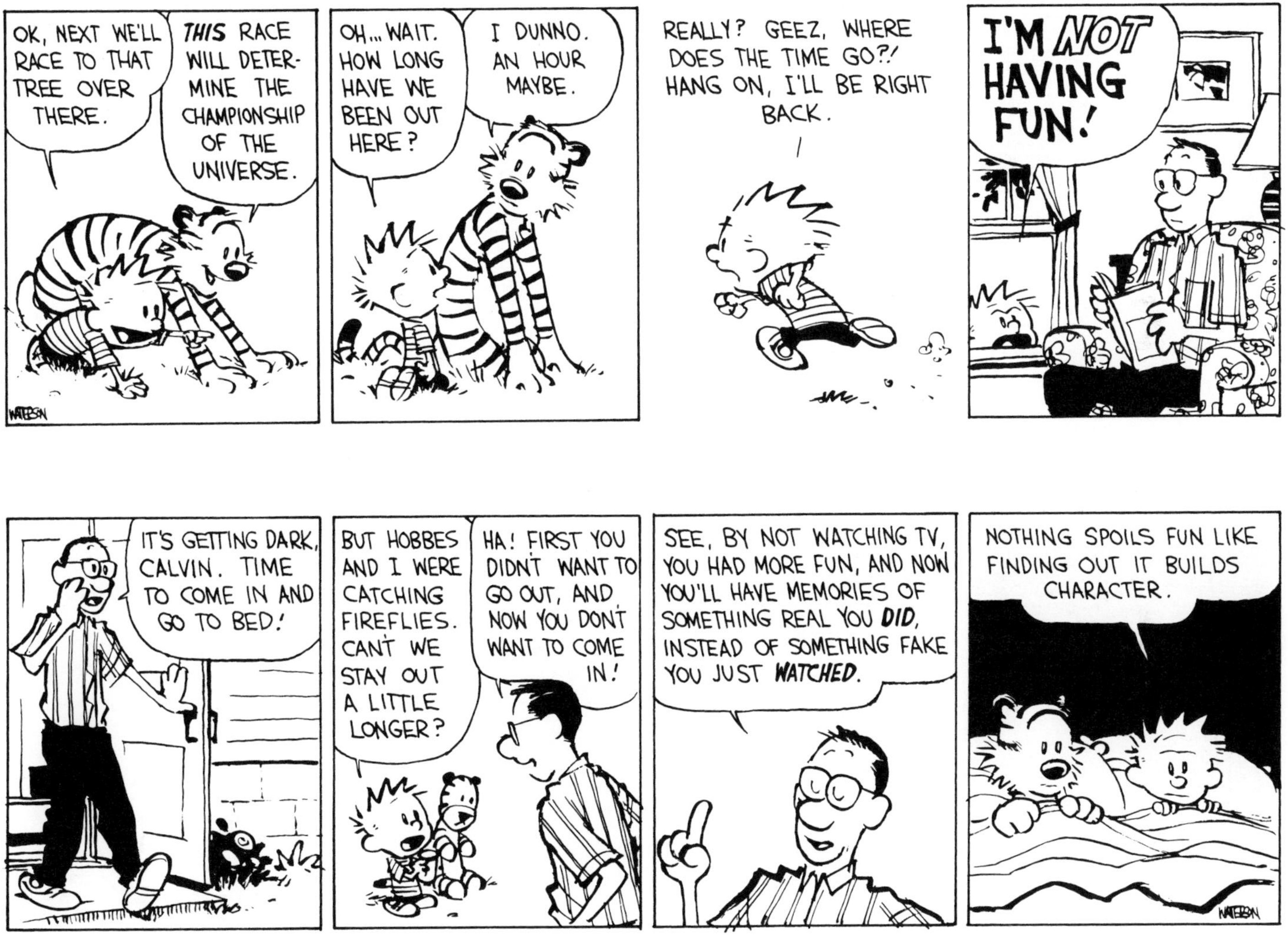
OK, NEXT WE'LL RACE TO THAT TREE OVER THERE.
THIS RACE WILL DETERMINE THE CHAMPIONSHIP OF THE UNIVERSE.
OH... WAIT. HOW LONG HAVE WE BEEN OUT HERE?
I DUNNO. AN HOUR MAYBE.
REALLY? GEEZ, WHERE DOES THE TIME GO?! HANG ON, I'LL BE RIGHT BACK.
I'M NOT HAVING FUN!
IT'S GETTING DARK, CALVIN. TIME TO COME IN AND GO TO BED!
BUT HOBBES AND I WERE CATCHING FIREFLIES. CAN'T WE STAY OUT A LITTLE LONGER?
HA! FIRST YOU DIDN'T WANT TO GO OUT, AND NOW YOU DON'T WANT TO COME IN!
SEE, BY NOT WATCHING TV, YOU HAD MORE FUN, AND NOW YOU'LL HAVE MEMORIES OF SOMETHING REAL YOU DID, INSTEAD OF SOMETHING FAKE YOU JUST WATCHED.
NOTHING SPOILS FUN LIKE FINDING OUT IT BUILDS CHARACTER.

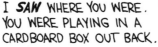

Calvin and Hobbes is distributed internationally by Andrews McMeel Syndication.

Andrews McMeel Publishing
a division of Andrews McMeel Universal
1130 Walnut Street, Kansas City, Missouri 64106

www.andrewsmcmeel.com

25 26 27 28 29 SDB 10 9 8 7 6 5 4 3 2 1

ISBN: 978-1-5248-9061-2

Library of Congress Control Number: 2024943648

ATTENTION: SCHOOLS AND BUSINESSES
Andrews McMeel books are available at quantity discounts with bulk purchase for educational, business, or sales promotional use.
For information, please e-mail the Andrews McMeel Publishing Special Sales Department: sales@amuniversal.com.